God to go outside and see how he might meet you in his great cathedral - his creation.

There are a great many good reasons for worshipping outside, but these are some of the most important ones:

Entering Into God's Imagination

As the John O'Donohue quote highlights, when we are outdoors we get to experience a world sprung straight out of God's imagination. We are surrounded by trees, flowers and creatures which are covered with the fingerprints of God the Creator. The changing seasons speak of life, growth, death and new life, and the more you learn about natural processes the more amazed and in awe you will be. Even if you actively resist it, you cannot help but learn about God - and perhaps even meet with God - in the natural environment, even if that is something as vague as a sense of wordless wonder.

The Bible Happened Outdoors

From Moses crossing the Red Sea, to Elijah standing in the mouth of a cave; from Jesus teaching about birds and flowers on the hillside, to the triumphant waving of palm branches when he entered Jerusalem; Scripture is stuffed full of events happening in nature as well as references to natural things. God is revealed in fire and in smoke, likened to a dove, a mother hen and streams of living water. It follows that immersing ourselves in God's creation will help us when we open the Bible.

We Feel Better Outdoors

Many studies (for example see this from Harvard Health: *engageworship.org/HarvardHealth*) have shown that our mental health is improved by being in a natural environment. Green plants make us calmer and slow our heart rate. Flowing water soothes our minds. Looking up at a huge tree or a wide horizon sparks awe and wonder. Perhaps it's a sense of perspective gained, perhaps it gives us the silence we need for processing, or perhaps it's because of the sense of God's presence.

We live in a time when mental health is an issue not just for the few, but for almost all of us. We have had to process the fallout of Covid-19, of too much time spent indoors on screens, of social upheaval and personal tragedies. And although the problems may be contemporary, the answers are ancient. "He leads me beside still waters," writes the psalmist, "he restores my soul" (Ps 23:2-3). Or consider Jesus, regularly taking himself out of the towns and cities and into wild places to pray (Luke 5:16), or

spending time on ⟨...⟩ got too much (Matt ⟨.....⟩ ⟨...⟩ ⟨...⟩ during his darkest hour (Mark 14:32).

Children Engage Outdoors

Our experience of Park Church has shown us that most often children are calmer, happier and more engaged in a natural environment. Perhaps it has to do with the space to roam, the noise of their shouts dissipating, or - again - perhaps it's the sensed presence of a creative and playful Creator. Studies show that children are some of the worst affected by "nature deficit disorder", and that getting away from screens and artificial light and into green, open spaces can bring most benefits to the young (see for example the work of Richard Louv: *engageworship.org/Louv*).

We have loved how truly "all-age" outdoor worship feels. There is no sense that a particular age group is higher in the pecking order. Sure, some adults may know some bird names - encourage them to share. But can they climb up into the tree where the bird just sat? We are often asked about ideas of how to best lead all-age worship. Although we can come up with many creative ideas for indoor worship, going outside is, in our experience, the best way to be truly intergenerational.

Blurring the Boundaries

Nature belongs to everyone. In the woods there is no scary threshold to step over if you're just exploring faith. We've welcomed people of all kinds of backgrounds and stages into outdoor worship gatherings, people who may find going into a church building very difficult. And we've got into conversations with other users of the park - dog walkers, picnicking families, the Muslim lady on the bench, the nature lover - all interested in why we're meeting in that place.

Blurring these boundaries is also helpful for those of us who have been Christians for a long time. It reminds us that God is not just to be found in "sacred" spaces, at prayer meetings or official church events. If we learn to meet with God in the park or the woods, we are perhaps more likely to meet him on our walk to work, in the town centre shops, or at school. It blurs the boundaries between "spiritual" and "leisure" activities, helping us see God in everyday things like playing games, learning facts, caring for nature and laughing together.

Caring for Creation

Last but certainly not least, worshipping in God's creation gives us a fresh appreciation of the gift that it is. We see its beauty, and its fragility. We realise the failure of humanity to care for God's world as he calls us to. And just as no healthy Christian would trash their church building, we are also inspired to look after this planet in new ways. Show your group how to tread lightly in your outdoor space, picking up litter and avoiding damaging plants and habitats, and these instincts should spill over into how they live all week.

We are privileged to have Jeremy and Louise Williams as part of our Park Church team. They bring a wealth of experience in living ecological lifestyles, campaigning for change, and educating others through books, radio and blogging (see *www.theearthbound.report*). We are sure that there are people in your church or community who would be thrilled to share their experiences with your group.

PRACTICALITIES

Hopefully you have caught some of our heart for worshipping outdoors. Before you jump in, here are a few more practical considerations as you start to lead your own gatherings:

Adapt the Activities

Read ahead through each week's material, and think about how you can adapt it for the size, age range and personalities of your group. Pay particular attention to any physical or learning needs, which might mean altering some activities dramatically or offering accessible alternatives. Don't feel that you need to do every activity we've suggested. And be very careful with health and safety considerations in your context, especially in the months when we are still emerging from the Covid-19 pandemic.

Adapt the Language

Secondly, think about your church tradition, and whether you need to adapt any of the language or spiritual styles for your group. There may be core practices such as saying the Lord's Prayer or a Confession which you want to add each time you meet. You might have people who are passionate about singing, so you could find ways to include more songs (we have sometimes taken a ukulele into the woods, drummed on fallen trees, and sung call-and-response songs which require no printed or projected words).

Play, Movement and Discussion

One of the joys of outdoor worship is blurring the boundaries between play, nature activities and spirituality. Consider the games, physical movements and quizzes a chance to grow in relationships, have fun and also discover something new about God's world. Indoor church isn't always so good at allowing a range of emotions or providing whole-body worshipping activities, so take the opportunity when you're meeting outside to laugh until your belly aches and stretch wide without the risk of poking someone in the eye. Enjoy!

FINALLY...

There are six category symbols to help you see at a glance what kind of activity each idea is - see the bottom of this page. We are also providing downloadable, printable PDFs, including the Bible passages to be read aloud. Access these at *engageworship.org/woods*

Lots of the ideas in this book have come out of actual Sunday morning meetings in the park and will have been shaped and changed by the community as we've explored together. So our thanks go to our friends whose thoughts and ideas may well lie unattributed within, not least Louise Williams, but also the Cheangs and the Flannagans. Thanks for all your creativity!

Trees

This session is a good introduction to worshipping in the woods. We will think about God as a gardener and get an overview of God's particular interest in trees. We will also use the beautiful age rings of a tree to think and pray about our own life and growth.

GATHERING

Praise With Psalm 96

Ask each member of your group to choose a tree they can see and try to form themselves like that tree - their bodies being the angle of the trunk and their arms showing where the branches reach. Praise God using Psalm 96. Alternatively, just read the psalm and reflect on the trees around you.

Reader: Sing to the Lord a new song;
sing to the Lord, all the earth.
Sing to the Lord, praise his name;
proclaim his salvation day after day.

Leader: Imagine trees singing praise - what would they sound like? Let's try to make some whooshy, swishy tree-singing sounds!

Reader: Declare his glory among the nations,
his marvellous deeds among all peoples.
For great is the Lord and most worthy of praise;
he is to be feared above all gods.
For all the gods of the nations are idols,
but the Lord made the heavens.

Leader: Look around you - what amazing things can you see? Point to them with your branches!

Reader: Splendour and majesty are before him;
strength and glory are in his sanctuary.
Ascribe to the Lord, all you families of nations,
ascribe to the Lord glory and strength.
Ascribe to the Lord the glory due to his name;
bring an offering and come into his courts.

Leader: Imagine bringing a gift to King Jesus on his throne - what would that look like in your tree form? Perhaps sway into a bow?

Reader: Worship the Lord in the splendour of his holiness;
tremble before him, all the earth.
Say among the nations, 'The Lord reigns.'
The world is firmly established, it cannot be moved;
he will judge the peoples with equity.

Leader: Can you tremble before our holy and mighty God? Perhaps shake your branches.

Reader: Let the heavens rejoice,
let the earth be glad;
let the sea resound, and all that is in it.
Let the fields be jubilant, and everything in them;
let all the trees of the forest sing for joy.

Leader: Can you be a jubilant rejoicing tree? Perhaps add some happy tree songs?

Reader: Let all creation rejoice before the Lord, for he comes, he comes to judge the earth. He will judge the world in righteousness and the peoples in his faithfulness.

Everyone: Amen!

TEACHING

Genesis 1 Reflection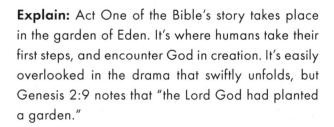

Explain: Act One of the Bible's story takes place in the garden of Eden. It's where humans take their first steps, and encounter God in creation. It's easily overlooked in the drama that swiftly unfolds, but Genesis 2:9 notes that "the Lord God had planted a garden."

The poetic creation account in Genesis 1 describes God calling plants and animals into being, but chapter 2 suggests something more careful and intentional. The garden, home to the creatures that will carry the divine image, has been created with special attention. It has been designed and planted. Right from the start, God is a gardener.

Ask: God puts trees in his garden - can you remember any specific trees mentioned in the Bible?

Explain: The Bible stories took place in the Middle East. As this area is a dry region, trees are a sign of water, fertility and blessing. Reflecting these conditions, the Bible often uses trees to illustrate

peace and provision. Righteous people are like trees planted by streams. A time of prosperity is imagined where people sit in the shade of their own fruit trees. And often, God is the one planting them. "I will plant trees in the barren desert" God tells Isaiah in a promise of restoration. To be precise, God says they will be "cedar, acacia, myrtle, olive, cypress, fir and pine," showing once again the divine abundance and diversity of nature (Isaiah 41:19).

Ask: Can you think of why trees are good to have in nature?

Explain: Trees provide shade and shelter. They provide a perch for birds, roots for burrowing animals. They host mosses and climbers, and are home to countless insects. Trees are a source of food and materials, and they cast their many benefits widely. We never know quite who is going to be blessed by a tree, especially one that lives for hundreds of years and well beyond the lifetime of the planter.

It's no surprise then that Jesus compared his kingdom to an expanding tree, in which the birds find a home. Or that Jesus invited us to see ourselves as branches in a vine. Or that Revelation describes the tree of life that stands in the city of heaven, another place planted and prepared for the people God loves.

God is a tree planter. When we plant trees, we are doing God's work. When we are in the woods, we are in God's presence.

Trees of the Bible Quiz

Run this quiz for the whole group where anyone who knows the answer can put their hand up, or divide into teams and write answers on paper. To make it easier, we have given the first letter of each tree. You could omit that and give the Bible reference instead, but that will take longer.

1. What kind of tree beginning with "O" does Absalom get stuck in by his hair in 2 Samuel 18?
A. Oak tree (2 Sam 18:9).

2. What wood beginning with "C" was Solomon's temple mostly built from?
A. Cedar (1 Kings 6:9).

3. What kind of tree beginning with "A" does the woman compare the man to in the love poem of the Songs of Solomon?
A. An apple tree among the trees of the forest (Song of Songs 2:3).

4. What tree beginning with "P" decorates the walls of the temple in Ezekiel's heavenly vision of chapter 40?
A. Palm trees (Ezekiel 40:16).

5. As well as being a shepherd before God calling him to prophesy, what trees beginning with "S" was Amos the caretaker of?
A. Sycamore trees (Amos 7:14).

6. What unfortunate tree beginning with "F" does Jesus curse, causing it to wither within that same day?
A. Fig tree (Mark 11:13).

7. What tree beginning with "M" does Jesus say that anyone with faith as small as a mustard seed can tell to uproot themselves and fling themselves into the sea?
A. Mulberry tree (Luke 17:6).

8. What tree beginning with "S" did Zacchaeus climb to see Jesus better in Jericho?
A. Sycamore tree (Luke 19:4).

9. What kind of tree beginning with "F" did Nathanael sit under when Jesus spotted him and then called him to be his disciple?
A. Fig tree (John 1:48).

10. Which plant beginning with "T" is voted king of the trees in a rather strange story in the book of Judges?
A. Thorn bush/Bramble (Judges 9:14).

Tree Rings

If there is a newly felled tree where you meet, or you're able to find a cut wood "disk" from a tree trunk, look at these as you speak. Otherwise, you may want to show a printed picture. Make sure you have some kind of wood for people to hold, look at and trace the lines with their fingers. Anything made from wood will show the tree ring texture, but depending on how the tree trunk was cut into planks, the rings may look like lines rather than rings.

Ask: Does anybody know how you can work out the age of a tree that has been felled?

Explain: When you cut a tree trunk, the rings you see indicate how old the tree is. Scientists - called dendrochronologists, try saying that fast! - can discover things about the environment during the different phases of the tree's life by examining the rings. Each band represents one year of growth. If scientists want to accurately measure a tree's age without harming it, they can use special boring machines that take out a core from the tree about the width of pencil lead. Using this method, some Bristlecone trees in Eastern California have been dated as being nearly 5000 years old!

Show on wood or picture as you explain: The light band is the spring wood made of large cells which grew when the weather was wet.

The dark band is the summer wood made of small cells formed when there was less rain. The two bands look different because the small cells of summer absorb more light and therefore look darker.

Some tree rings are wide and some are narrow. Wide rings form during a year when the weather was very good for growth, such as warm and wet. Narrow rings form during drier years and cooler years.

You can also see if the tree has been damaged during its growth, if there's been some trauma like a forest fire or other damage.

RESPONSE

Tree Rings *Examen*

You will need: A copy each of the downloadable illustration, as well as a pen each. Depending on where you are meeting, clipboards (or thick cardboard and pegs) might be helpful too.

Lead this prayer time slowly, giving enough space for everyone to draw and write. If you have small children in your group, the space and quiet will need to be interspersed with chatting about what you're drawing:

If you were a tree, what story would your rings tell about how you have grown over the years? Let's use tree rings to help us reflect.

Take a sheet. The middle dot is when you were born, and the outer bark is today. Draw circles for each year of your life (or, if you are a little older, perhaps draw them in 5 year gaps). Now write down significant events, experiences and relationships from your life in those gaps.

Which of those events are you grateful to God for? Talk to him about those.

Which of those things hold regrets, hurts or disappointments? Talk to God about those too. God sees all of your past, he wants us to bring it all to him.

How have you grown and developed over the years? What would you say to your younger self? Where do you feel God is encouraging you to grow next?

SENDING

Oaks Of Righteousness

You will need: *a measuring tape, a Bible or print-out of the text.*

Gather near the biggest tree you can find in your space, ideally an oak tree. You can't see it's rings, but here's a simple way to estimate the tree's age:

Measure around the trunk of the tree (the girth) at about 1m from the ground.

Then divide the girth in centimetres by 2.5 to give an age in years (for example: a tree with a 50cm girth will be about 20 years old).

Trees grow at different rates, an oak grows slowly, so for a more exact age, divide the girth by 1.88. Pine trees grow fast, so if you've measured one of those, divide the girth by 3.13.

Marvel at the age of your tree, and think about the historical dates that this mighty tree was present for.

Next, ask someone to read this:

> "The Spirit of the Sovereign Lord is on me...
> to comfort all who mourn,
> and provide for those who grieve in Zion –
> to bestow on them a crown of beauty
> instead of ashes,
> the oil of joy instead of mourning,
> and a garment of praise
> instead of a spirit of despair.
> They will be called oaks of righteousness,
> a planting of the Lord
> for the display of his splendour."
> (Isaiah 61:1a, 2b-3)

Discuss: What "instead of's" did you hear in that passage?

Explain: Whatever struggles we have seen in our past as we looked at our "tree rings", God has promised to be with us and to help us grow through those difficult times. In this passage he promises to use his people to bring comfort to those who grieve, joy to those who mourn and praise instead of despair. God's plan for us is to grow us into "oaks of righteousness", magnificent, strong and healthy trees, showing God's style to the world around us.

Teach the phrase "Fill us with your Spirit, God". You might want to include a hand action, such as miming a jug pouring on our heads, or rain coming down.

All: Fill us with your Spirit, God,
Leader: to comfort all who mourn.
All: Fill us with your Spirit, God,
Leader: to bring beauty where there's ashes.
All: Fill us with your Spirit, God,
Leader: to bring joy instead of mourning.
All: Fill us with your Spirit, God,
Leader: to bring praise instead of despair.
All: Fill us with your Spirit, God,
Leader: grow us into oaks of righteousness,
for the display of your splendour.
All: Amen.

Light

WEEK TWO

Trees and plants grow towards the light. This session investigates this in the wild, and looks at how we can "grow towards the light" in our faith.

GATHERING

Joyful, Joyful 🔲

Ask the group to stand in a circle, and to imagine that the sun is in the centre.

Explain: In the hymn "Joyful, joyful", the writer (Henry Van Dyke) imagines that God is like the sun.

The writer is not worshipping the sun, but he is being poetic in picturing God as the source of light, warmth and joy for everything in creation - the centre of our universe which everything orbits around.

Read out these two verses of the hymn, and perhaps invite the group to make up an action to sum up each line (making sure to read slowly enough).

Alternatively, if you can make the words available, you may want to simply sing these two verses together (to the tune of "Ode To Joy").

Joyful, joyful, we adore you,
God of glory, Lord of love;
hearts unfold like flowers before you,
opening to the sun above.
Melt the clouds of sin and sadness;
drive the dark of doubt away;
giver of immortal gladness,
fill us with the light of day!

All your works with joy surround you,
earth and heaven reflect your rays,
stars and angels sing around you,
centre of unbroken praise;
field and forest, vale and mountain,
flowery meadow, flashing sea,
chanting bird and flowing fountain
praising you eternally!

Exploring Trees and Light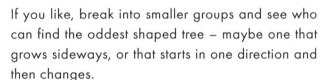

Discuss: What do you think a tree needs to thrive?

Explain: A tree wants to draw up nutrients from the ground, and it wants to catch light from the sun through its leaves. It will grow in the best possible shape to do those things, from whatever place it finds itself.

Go for a walk and look at the many ways that the trees have grown. Look at how the trunks rise towards the sun. See how the branches reach out towards gaps between the other trees. Can you see any trees that are bigger on one side than the other? Or that have bent away from the shade? Often trees have more branches and leaves facing south, where there is more sun.

The Shapes of a Tree

If you like, break into smaller groups and see who can find the oddest shaped tree – maybe one that grows sideways, or that starts in one direction and then changes.

Since trees take decades to grow, there is often a story in these trees that we can only guess at. Perhaps the tree has been shaped by the availability of light, or by the wind, or by an accident – or if it's in a park, it might have been deliberately cut by people.

Take a few minutes to sketch the shape of the tree. As you do so, see if you can work out why it grew that way. You could take photos of the trees if you prefer.

Share your drawing or photos when you meet back together again. Who found the strangest shaped tree?

Leaning Like a Tree

Explain: Plants move towards the light. This is called "phototropism", and you might have noticed this if you've ever grown seedlings or a pot plant on a windowsill. All living creatures are made up of cells, and one way that plants bend is by growing their cell walls longer on the shady side. That tips them in the other direction.

We can try this ourselves. Stand up straight with your feet together, and then try to make yourself longer on one side. As you feel your skin and muscles stretch on one side, did you bend the other way? Who can bend the furthest to one side without moving their feet?

When you bend too far, you start to tip over. You will instinctively move your foot out to balance yourself. Trees do this too, in slow motion. As they bend in one direction at the top, they will send out roots to keep themselves balanced.

How much further can you bend to the side if you spread your legs a little wider?

TEACHING

Belonging to the Light

Explain: Leaves are like little solar panels for trees, and the tree puts a huge amount of effort into getting those solar panels into the best possible position. They love the light. The more they can get, the bigger they will grow. They put all their effort into reaching for more light.

In 1 Thessalonians chapter 5, the Apostle Paul is writing to a church that is having a bit of a hard time. He reassures them using the example of light:

> "For you are all children of the light and of the day; we don't belong to darkness and night. So be on your guard, not asleep like the others. Stay alert and be clearheaded. Night is the time when people sleep and drinkers get drunk. But let us who live in the light be clearheaded, protected by the armour of faith and love, and wearing as our helmet the confidence of our salvation.
>
> For God chose to save us through our Lord Jesus Christ, not to pour out his anger on us. Christ died for us so that, whether we are dead or alive when he returns, we can live with him forever. So encourage each other and build each other up, just as you are already doing." (1 Thess 5: 5-11 NLT)

Discuss: What do you think it means to "belong to the light"?

What kind of people do you think "children of the light" would be?

Reaching for the Light

If a tree wants light and reaches up towards it, perhaps we could think of a person of light as someone who reaches towards God. If a tree catches sunlight and turns it into growth, perhaps we could imagine a person of light catching the light of God and turning it into energy for doing good things in the world. As they get older, they

grow out towards God and understand more and more about him.

Reflect (in small groups or personally):

- How could we "position" ourselves towards God's light?

- How can we catch God's love and pass it on to those around us?

- How can we use our energy to make good things happen in the world?

- Share/reflect on what you are already doing, and where God might be leading you.

RESPONSE

Active Confession Prayer

Lead each action with the simple instructions in the square brackets, giving enough time for everyone to move and also to reflect the spoken prayer in their hearts.

Explain: We are going to respond to God using a prayer with actions.

[Start turned away from the sun]

Pray: God, we are sorry when we turn away from you. Sometimes it's because we're selfish, sometimes it's because we're stressed, but right now, in the silence, we confess this to you.

[Turn back towards the sun]

Pray: We repent, turn back, aim to direct ourselves towards you, God. Thank you for your forgiveness in Christ.

[Cover your eyes with your hands]

Pray: Sometimes we find ourselves in the dark, Lord. Obstacles, depression or confusion descend on us. It can be a scary time, but we thank you that Psalm 23 says:

> "Even though I walk through the darkest valley,
> I will fear no evil, for you are with me;
> your rod and your staff, they comfort me."

Thank you for your presence with us in the dark places. May we be like the plants that grow the most in these times, and reach for you with all our might.

[Remove your hands]

Pray: God, your love is amazing, blinding and stunning. We wait in your presence now.

SENDING

Active Sending Prayer

After pausing to allow people to wait in God's presence for as long as you think appropriate, you can flow into this final prayer.

Explain: To finish our time we're going to pray using our bodies again, this time growing from a small seed into a tree that catches God's light.

[Crouch down into a ball, like an acorn or conker]

Pray: God, we're very small, and don't always understand everything. Please keep us safe.

[From a crouch, raise a hand, like a little shoot]

Pray: God, as we go out into the world, help us to be brave.

[Rising a little, spread fingers wide above head, like you've got some leaves poking out]

Pray: God, let us grow strong in your love.

[Stand up, arms bent at the elbow, like branches reaching out]

Pray: God, give us your light. Help us to turn it into energy to do good things in the world.

[Reach arms up, making yourself as big as you can, to catch all the sun you can]

Pray: God, help us to catch more and more of your light. Amen.

Roots

WEEK THREE

In this session we look at roots, and the amazing ways they help trees and plants. We explore what it means to be rooted in the love of God as well as in the Bible.

GATHERING

Jesus' Love Action Poem

Explain that you will say a line and do an action, and invite everyone to repeat after you.

This is based on Ephesians 3:17-18.

No love is wider, [*Stretch out arms to the side*]
no love is longer, [*Stretch front and back*]
so root us God [*Stamp down feet*]
in the love of Jesus. [*Make a heart with your hands*]

No love is higher, [*Stretch arms up*]
no love is deeper, [*Get as low as you can*]
so root us God [*Stamp down feet*]
in the love of Jesus. [*Make a heart with your hands*]

Roots Activity

Find a place where you can see a lot of tree roots. Some hills and banks reveal root structures under trees, or you might be able to find a tree that has fallen over and is showing its roots.

Spend some time looking at the root structure and talking about what you see. You could draw the roots in your notebook, or take photos of them.

Explain: Most of the time we can't see tree roots, they are hidden under the ground but they are vital to the tree.

Discuss: Can you think of other things which are hidden but very important?

(For example: Icebergs mostly under water, water pipes under the ground, vital organs in our bodies, people who do important jobs but are rarely seen by the public)

Explain: The radius of the tree is the distance between the middle of the trunk and its furthest out branch. Can you spot the furthest out branch of the tree you are looking at? Roots will often grow out between 2 and 5 times further than the furthest branch. Try to imagine how far away the furthest root might be if it was twice the length, or five times the length of that furthest branch!

Discuss: What do you think the purpose of the roots is?

Explain: There are three basic things tree roots do:

1. Absorb water
2. Absorb nutrients (the tree's food)
3. Hold the plant steady in the ground

Balance Game

Give everyone in the group a particular posture to stand in: ask some to stand slightly wide-legged, feet pointing outwards a little bit; ask some others to stand with their feet and legs pressed together; some to stand on one leg and some to sit in a squat.

Next, play a game such as catch using a ball or a frisbee, "Simon Says", "Zip, Zap, Boing" or any other game that your group is used to playing.

If you want to make it competitive (which would perhaps be a little unfair as some have harder postures to maintain!), anyone who falls over or changes their posture is 'out' until one solid champion remains.

Discuss:

- Which posture was hardest to maintain?
- Which posture was best for balance?
- Which posture is most like the roots of a tree?
- What would happen if a tree had roots like our one-foot stance or squat posture?

TEACHING

Roots Down Deep

Read: Ask different people to read out these Bible passages:

"Let your roots grow down into [Jesus], and let your lives be built on him. Then your faith will grow strong in the truth you were taught, and you will overflow with thankfulness." (Col 2:7)

"Then Christ will make his home in your hearts as you trust in him. Your roots will grow down into God's love and keep you strong." (Eph 3:17)

Discuss:

- Why do you think that Paul, the writer of these verses, used the image of roots?

- What might it mean to let our roots go deep into Jesus? Compare with the three purposes of tree roots referenced above (absorbing water and nutrients, and to hold the tree steady).

Then ask someone to read this saying from Jesus:

"The seed falling on rocky ground refers to someone who hears the word and at once receives it with joy. But since they have no root, they last only a short time. When trouble or persecution comes because of the word, they quickly fall away." (Matt 13:20-21)

Explain: Here, Jesus warns that if people don't have their roots in his word, they will struggle to keep going for God when hard times come.

Discuss: What would it practically look like to be rooted in God's word? [*For example: Reading the Bible, praying, spending time with other Christians, living God's ways.*]

RESPONSE/SENDING

Rooted in God

Engage with this prayer and the actions as you are physically able. If the balancing postures are too taxing, you could give the option to use the left palm and the first two fingers on the right hand to represent the ground and legs.

Begin by standing on one leg with the other foot resting on the opposite leg's ankle, calf or even thigh if you're feeling flexible (not on your knee or you might hurt yourself).

Pray: Father God, we're sorry when we are not well rooted in you. We are sorry when we rely more on ourselves than on you. We know that we need your love to feed and grow us.

Explain: Lets take a moment in silence to confess in our hearts times when we have relied more on ourselves than on God. [*Pause*]

Next, stand on one leg, the other leg bent at 90 degrees by the knee and lifted so that the thigh is 90 degrees from the torso.

Pray: When we forget to keep ourselves rooted in your love, God, we feel out of balance and unsteady.

Explain: In the silence, tell God about an area of your life where you feel unsteady and out of balance. [*Pause*]

Finally, stand with both your feet flat on the ground, as firmly as you can.

Pray: Thank you for your invitation, God, to grow our roots into your love. Help us feel your love as clearly as we feel the ground under our feet. Help us welcome your love and power into our lives, to sustain us, and to keep us steady as we leave this place. Amen.

Fungi

WEEK FOUR

In this session we learn about fungi, that they are more than the mushrooms we put in food and how fungi provide a connective network for the woods. We explore what the Bible tells us about our connection to one another and how we can be community together.

GATHERING

In the Darkest Places

Explain: In a previous session we thought about light, and what it means to be "children of the light". However, the Bible uses images like this in multi-layered ways. In Psalm 74 it says:

> "Both day and night belong to you;
> you made the starlight and the sun."
> (Ps 74:16 NLT)

This psalm reminds us that although people can misuse darkness for bad purposes, originally God made the night-time as a good thing. Night is a time when our bodies and the natural world can grow and heal, a time for rest and preparation for the next day. Some people are afraid of the dark, but we can know that God is always with us, even in dark places. In another psalm it says:

> "If I say, 'Surely the darkness will hide me
> and the light become night around me,'
> even the darkness will not be dark to you;
> the night will shine like the day,
> for darkness is as light to you." (Ps 139:11-12)

Today we're going to be thinking about Fungi, which mostly live in dark places - underground or in shaded areas. Let's say this prayer to open our session; you say "In the darkest places" and I'll respond with a line. [*You could invite the group to put their hands over their eyes.*]

In the darkest places:
We need not be afraid.
In the darkest places:
God's love is still displayed.
In the darkest places:
Things will grow without us knowing.
In the darkest places:
see God's glory softly glowing.

In the darkest places:
There is peace and restoration.
In the darkest places:
There is hope for all creation.
In the darkest places:
We don't need to be afraid.
In the darkest places:
Jesus meets us every day.

Fungus Quiz

You could run this quiz together as a larger group encouraging people to put their hand up to answer, or you could divide into teams and make it competitive.

1. True or False: Fungi are plants?
A. False: from the 1960s onwards scientists have thought of fungi as a different category or "kingdom" of organisms alongside plants and animals.

2. What type of fungus helps us to make bread and wine?
A. Yeast is a fungus.

3. Are fungi good for us or harmful?
A. Trick question - Both! We can eat mushrooms and truffles. Medicines like the antibiotic penicillin can be produced by a fungus, but some fungi are toxic and harmful to humans, such as when mould grows on your food.

4. The "Encyclopedia of Biodiversity" names 75,000 species of fungi, but scientists believe that many more unnamed species exist. Do you think those 75,000 are 50%, 20% or 5% of the estimated amount of species?
A. Just 5%.

5. How could a mushroom help you see in the dark?
A. Over 30 species of mushroom glow, a chemical reaction called bioluminescence.

6. What is biggest - the blue whale, a group of aspen trees in Utah, or honey fungus in Oregon?

A. The honey fungus is bigger in distance, covering 1350 football fields, but the aspen trees are heavier weighing more than 65 blue whales.

7. Could you think of a way fungus could help you find your way out of an Ikea store?
A. A curious scientist once made a model of Ikea and put a fungus in the middle to see if it could find its way out. Because fungus can grow in every direction at once, it easily found the shortest way to the exit.

8. True or false: Some fungi are strong enough to break through tarmac.
A. Correct. Fungi grow by sending out tiny threads called hyphae, which are incredibly strong and can crack through tarmac roads. If a hypha was as wide as a human arm, it could lift a bus.

Finding Fungi

Try to find some fungi in the area where you are meeting. If it's autumn and you are meeting in the woods, it might be fairly easy to find large fungi, which we often lazily call mushrooms. Get help with identifying your fungi on this web page: engagworship.org/WoodlandTrust

Marvel at the amazing names and shapes of these remarkable creatures.

Fungi love feeding off dying wood, so if there's a half-rotten log somewhere in your area, this would be a good place to start looking. Perhaps look at what other living things you can find in the dead wood (mosses, insects, lichens and so on) and marvel at how a tree that has "died" continues to support life in this way.

TEACHING

Wood Wide Web

[If you find this interesting, you might want to watch Suzanne Simard's TED talk here - engageworship.org/simard]

Ask: Do you know what the connection between computers, smartphones and tablets is called?

Explain: We use terms like "the Internet" and the "world wide web" to describe how computers talk to one another, sharing information across countries and the world. But did you know that a long time before the world wide web, fungi have provided trees with their own "wood wide web"?

A scientist called Suzanne Simard has researched this dark, hidden world. She explains that tree roots are connected under the ground by threads of fungus called mycelium, in networks that span across whole forests. She says:

> "The web is so dense that there can be hundreds of kilometres of mycelium under a single footstep. And not only that, mycelium connects different individuals in the forest, individuals not only of the same species but between species, like birch and fir, and it works kind of like the Internet."
> (TED talk)

What is amazing is that this underground network allows trees to share carbon dioxide, nitrogen, phosphorus, water, and not just that but also defence signals to warn other trees of danger. Old hub trees or "mother trees", often hundreds of years old, can be connected to hundreds of other trees, helping them to grow by sharing resources and "forest wisdom" with them.

Suzanne and other scientists have discovered that if you remove too many of these "mother trees" from a forest, it can lead to disaster as the younger trees no longer have the wisdom and protection of the older trees to help them grow. They also saw that a diversity of different types of trees was helpful to a forest, that encouraging variety encouraged life and health in the woods.

Connections Game

You will need a ball of yarn for this game. Make sure it's big enough that the yarn doesn't run out too quickly.

Stand in a circle. The first person must hold firmly onto one end of the yarn and throw the ball to someone else in the circle (this takes quite a bit of coordination, so young children will need help!). The next person should keep a hold of the yarn and throw the ball to someone else, allowing it to unravel a little each time it's thrown. Continue to throw the ball of yarn until everyone is holding onto the yarn.

You will either be left with an attractive looking web of connection, or a knotted mess. If the latter, have a short discussion about what went wrong and how amazing it is that the woods can connect using fungi underground without getting knotted!

If you've had some success with your web, move on to the next activity. See if you can send a 'tug' through the string, that is, the last person who received the yarn tugs gently on the yarn leading to the person who threw it to them. See if you could reverse the throwing order using tugs. Perhaps try it with your eyes closed.

Discuss:

- How is your string like the "wood wide web"? [*It's connecting organisms using a string-like substance.*]

- How is it not like the "wood wide web"? [*It's only connected one organism to one other, rather than having many connections with different organisms. Imagine what a complicated web you'd have to create if you wanted everyone in the circle to have a direct connection with everyone else!*]

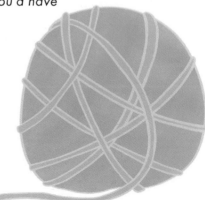

Made for Community

Explain: In a previous session, we thought of ourselves as individual trees with roots. But maybe this picture of the "wood wide web" connecting all the different trees in a forest might help us to think of ourselves as Christians who need to live in connection with others.

Read: Romans 16:1-15 together, either out loud as a whole group or in smaller groups [*if you have younger children you could cut this down or summarise*].

Explain: In this text Paul is greeting lots of different people who have worked with him in sharing the love of Jesus - his own Christian community.

Discuss:

- What do you notice about all these people? [*For example: lots of them, many different racial backgrounds, women and men...*]

- How do you think Paul felt about them?

You could also draw attention to Hebrews 11, where the writer lists people from history who followed God and inspired future generations of believers. The writer calls these a "cloud of witnesses" (Heb 12:1), or "all these pioneers who blazed the way, all these veterans cheering us on" (Heb 12:1 MSG).

Explain: The early church didn't think that their faith was a solo sport. They knew that they were part of a web of relationships, connected to other people who followed God, supporting and inspiring them.

RESPONSE

Web of Faith

Discuss: As our response, we're going to draw our own webs of faith. Who are the different people who support you in your Christian life? [*This could be in church, your family, friends or colleagues. It could be older or younger people*].

Explain: Draw a diagram of the "network" of different people who are part of the web of your faith [*something like this:*]

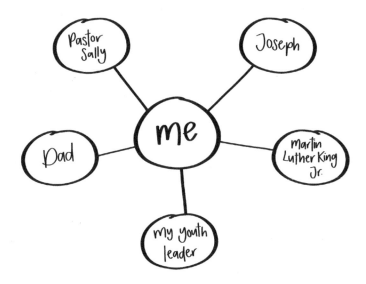

Discuss: Are there people from the past who inspire you; in the Bible, or other historical figures?

Add these historical figures to your web diagram. End the session by thanking God for the wider "web" of people who inspire, support and influence us today, either praying open prayers or using the active prayer below.

SENDING

Prayer

Stand in a circle and spread your legs so that your toes touch the next person's toes and you become like a connected network.

Think about one person who has supported you in your life of faith.

Pray: "Thank you God for _____".

Then think of one person that you could support in their faith, by encouraging them, listening to them, sharing with them or in some other way.

Pray: "God help me to support _____".

Leaves

WEEK FIVE

In this session we find out about leaves, how they bring life to the tree and how they change through the seasons. We then think about what the Bible teaches us about the rhythm and seasons of life.

GATHERING

Every Season

Teach the following song to the tune of "London's Burning":

Every season, every season,
God is with us, God is with us,
spring and summer, autumn, winter,
God's love is unceasing.

Explain: Songs often go in cycles, with a natural rhythm, a beginning and an end, but also a re-starting as the tune loops around.

Discuss:

- What other things in life go in cycles? [*For example: the week, the seasons of the year, the water cycle.*]

- What other things in life have rhythms? [*For example: heartbeat, walking, day and night.*]

Leaf Collecting

Go and find a variety of different leaves. Either pick them up from the ground, take pictures of them or draw them in a notebook (don't pull any leaves from plants).

Bring back your different leaves and try and describe how they look different.

If there are a lot of fallen leaves, you can have a competition to dress someone as a tree. In pairs, collect leaves and dress one person, then see who looks most like a tree.

TEACHING

Seasons in the Bible

Read: Ask people to read out these Bible passages:

"As long as the earth endures, seedtime and harvest, cold and heat, summer and winter, day and night will never cease." (Gen 8:22)

"It was you who set all the boundaries of the earth; you made both summer and winter." (Ps 74:17)

Explain: These verses describe God as the creator of the rhythms and cycles in the natural world.

Discuss:

- What is your favourite season of the year?
- What is your least favourite season?
- What season are we in now?
- What signs tell you that we're in that season?

The Leaf Cycle

[You may want to have some evergreen tree leaves and deciduous tree leaves there for your group to feel and compare during the discussion.]

Explain: Evergreen trees are green all year round, and their leaves are hardier, often waxy and thick, or pointy like needles. But as the seasons of the year turn, leaves on deciduous trees - that is non-evergreen - go on a cycle.

Discuss:

- When in the seasons do leaves begin to grow on trees? [Spring time.]

- What jobs do leaves do for trees? [Absorbing water, sunlight, carbon dioxide and oxygen. Protecting them from animals and harsh weather. Evaporating water to cool the plant when it is too hot.]

- When are the leaves at their greenest? [Summer time.]

- What makes the leaves green? [The tree produces chlorophyll, which reflects green light but absorbs red and blue. This is converted by photosynthesis into sugar and oxygen to help the plant grow.]

- What colours do the leaves start to go in the autumn? [Red, orange, yellow and brown. The tree stops sending chlorophyll to the leaves, so these are the natural colours of the leaves without chlorophyll in them.]

- Why does the tree do this? [Explain by asking what happens if you leave a closed glass bottle full of water in the freezer. It explodes, since water expands when it freezes. The same would happen in the leaf if it tried to stay on the tree, as the liquid in the leaf would expand and kill the leaf. Then the tree would be full of dead leaves that it wasted energy on and would receive no nutrients in return. Also, the damage might spread into the tree, putting the whole tree - not just the leaves - in danger. So the tree stops sending chlorophyll and then the leaves begin to drop off the tree.]

- What happens after the leaves fall, during winter time? [They are not wasted. The leaves that fall to the ground break down and become nutritious food for the roots of trees and plants. So when it is winter and the trees look bare, we can remember that there is lots of life and development going on under our feet. This process allows the cycle to begin again the next spring.]

Seasons in Life

Explain: Just as the leaves go through seasons, so we have different seasons in our lives. Some seasons we start new things, like nature does in spring.

Discuss: What are some new things we could be starting, or that you're starting right now? [*For example: new school, new job, learning a new skill, getting to know new people.*]

Explain: Other times are more like summer. This is a bright, happy time with lots of activity.

Discuss: Who feels like they're in a summer-like season of life?

Explain: Other times are like autumn, when there are all kinds of changes going on.

Discuss: Who has changes happening in their life? How does that feel?

Explain: And then some seasons of our life are like winter, when we're waiting, not much seems to be happening, things have ended and not yet re-started.

Discuss: Is anyone in a winter phase of life?

A Time For Every Season

Write out on card (or print out) these verses and separate the beginning and end of each line. Ask the group to try and pair them up.

a time to be born and	a time to die,
a time to plant and	a time to uproot,
a time to kill and	a time to heal,
a time to tear down and	a time to build,
a time to weep and	a time to laugh,
a time to mourn and	a time to dance,
a time to scatter stones and	a time to gather them,
a time to embrace and	a time to refrain from embracing,
a time to search and	a time to give up,
a time to keep and	a time to throw away,
a time to tear and	a time to mend,
a time to be silent and	a time to speak,
a time to love and	a time to hate,
a time for war and	a time for peace.

Discuss:

- This passage in Ecclesiastes 3 starts "There is a time for everything, and a season for every activity under the heavens" (Ecc 3:1). What do you think this means?

- Are there any of these "times" that you relate to right now? Or that make you think of people or situations?

- Some of these things are quite difficult and negative (kill, hate, war... etc). What do you think it means that there is "a time for" these things? How do you think God views those things?

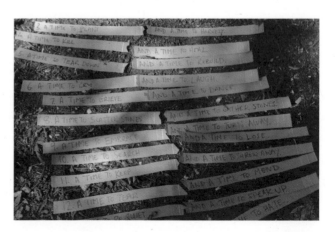

RESPONSE

Prayer for the Season

Discuss: In small groups or pairs, ask people to talk about this: If there is a "season" for everything, what season do you feel like you are in right now? Is it happy or sad, exciting or boring, secure or uncertain...? Share in the group about the season of life you feel you are in.

Pray: Pray for each other, that you would trust that God has good things for you during this season. If this season is hard, pray for strength and support to make it through this season with God.

SENDING

Leaves for Healing

Explain: To close, we are going to think a bit wider beyond ourselves, to pray for God's world.

Read: Ask someone to read this verse, explaining that it comes at the end of the Bible and is about God's future for the world:

> "On each side of the river stood the tree of life, bearing twelve crops of fruit, yielding its fruit every month. And the leaves of the tree are for the healing of the nations." (Rev 22:2)

If you've collected fallen leaves then use these. In spring or summer you might want to print out some leaf shapes, use ones that you've pruned off in your garden or draw them in your notebooks.

Think about one thing in the world which needs God's healing. Write that on your leaf, and then pray in small groups that God would bring his healing in those situations.

Seeds

WEEK SIX

This session helps us think about how nature spreads the seeds of different plants, and how this can inspire us to spread the love of God to our friends.

GATHERING

Psalm 126

In one psalm the writer says:

"Those who plant in tears
will harvest with shouts of joy.
They weep as they go to plant their seed,
but they sing as they return with the harvest."
(Ps 126:5-6 NLT)

Discuss: Talk as a group about things that are making you sad at the moment. That could be personal struggles, problems in your local area, things in the news or other issues.

Ask everyone to choose one of those things, and imagine that it is a seed in their hand. Bringing our sad things to God is like planting a seed. We may be sad as we plant that seed, we may even cry, or be angry, or experience some other emotions. But God promises that when we bring those things to him, and patiently wait for his response, we can look forward to a time when those prayers will be answered.

Read the verses again, and invite people to mime bending over to plant their seed and then jump up in praise.

Those who plant in tears
[*Bend over and mime planting seed, say your sadness to God*]
will harvest with shouts of joy.
[*Jump up and shout "praise God"*]
They weep as they go to plant their seed,
[*Repeat planting seed*]
but they sing as they return with the harvest.
[*Repeat jumping and shouting*]

Seeds Of Wonder

Before the session: Collect as many seeds and fruit grown from those seeds as you can; perhaps spend a week or so remembering to keep seeds back from the compost bin when you chop up fruit and vegetables. Easy ones would be seeds from apples, tomatoes, melons, pumpkins/squashes, avocados, chillies or peppers; harder ones (and most likely requiring purchasing some seeds) might be carrots, peas, lettuce or anything else you could think of where you can have access to both seed and produce.

Play a guessing game where you try to match the seed to the fruit; perhaps bring a large white sheet to put them all on.

Discuss: Once all seeds and produce are matched, talk about:

- Which is the smallest seed you can see?

- Which is the largest seed?

- Which is the smallest seed compared to its produce?

- What is the largest thing you've grown from a seed?

Explain: Isn't it amazing that these tiny seeds can grow and become plants that bear these kinds of fruit? In the case of an apple, for example, their tiny seeds don't just grow into an apple - that would be amazing enough, but into a whole tree that can bear many fruits. Wow!

Seeds in the Woods

What seeds can you find on the forest floor? For example, look out for conkers, acorns, sycamore seeds and beech nuts. Which trees do they come from?

Alternatively, find out what trees are in the area where you meet, and print out pictures of their respective seeds. See if you can match the seed with the tree, and then marvel over how something so large can come from something so small.

Follow the Seeds

Explain: A seed's job is to help a tree or plant to make more of itself — to become a new tree or plant. To do that, it needs to move to a new spot. How does it do that in the wild, since seeds don't have any legs?

Different seeds do this in different ways. See if you can find some examples of these in your woods today:

- Some seeds disperse on the wind, like sycamore and ash trees.

- Birds move some seeds around, by eating berries and pooping the seeds into new places.

- Squirrels take seeds and nuts and bury them. They forget some of them, and they can grow into new trees.

- Some seeds just drop and roll. There might not be any in your woods, but coconut palms drop their huge seeds and the sea moves them around.

- Seeds with burrs stick to passing animals, including people's coats, and then fall off elsewhere.

Tree Babies

See if you can find a tree with wind-blown seeds, such as an ash, sycamore, or birch. Start at the trunk and then walk outwards and see if you can find shoots, saplings or new trees that have come from this parent tree. Are there more in a certain direction? Could that reflect the prevailing wind?

Spreading Seeds

[Warning: very physically active!]

Mark out a space in your outdoor area where the game will take place (not too large, everyone needs to hear the leader) and check that it's free of dog mess and other things you don't want people to roll around in. Teach everyone the different actions first:

- "Dandelion seeds" - "blow around" the field, spin with your arms swaying in the wind.

- "Raspberry seeds" - pretend to be pooped out: sink to the ground with a wiggle.

- "Acorn" - pretend to be buried: drop to the ground and curl into a ball.

- "Coconut" - drop to the ground and roll, either on your side or using roly-polies.

- "Burdock" - "stick" to someone. Either grab onto someone's shoulders from the back, or if social distancing rules are in place, stand two metres behind someone else and pretend that your fingers are the burrs sticking to the person.

In between these actions, the leader can shout "spread" and everyone just has to run and be as evenly spread out in your area as possible. The leader can at any time shout any of the actions and all the players must obey by acting like that seed. If you want to make it competitive, failure to do the correct action or doing it too slowly could eliminate players until only one powerful seed remains!

TEACHING

Sowing the Seed

Explain: Jesus often uses the image of spreading seed as a picture of telling other people about God. We have seen that in nature, seeds are spread in lots of different ways. There are lots of ways we can spread the message of Jesus, through words and actions.

Discuss: What are some ways you can think of to share God's love with people you know?

[Examples: Telling a friend what God has done for you. Being kind to someone who is lonely. Offering to pray for someone. Inviting someone to a church event. Looking after God's creation...]

Ask people to stand in four groups, and give each group a section of the reading (Matt 13:3-4; 5-6; 7; 8.) Invite them to act out their section of the reading as one person speaks it out. They can have a couple of minutes to prepare, then have each group perform in order.

Discuss:

- What do you think Jesus meant by this parable?

- What does it mean to have "good soil"?

- What does it mean for us as people who are trying to share God's word? *[You may want to read Matt 13:18-23 where Jesus explains the parable, and then discuss further.]*

RESPONSE

Tiny Seeds

Read: Ask someone to read this passage:

> "He told them another parable: 'The kingdom of heaven is like a mustard seed, which a man took and planted in his field. Though it is the smallest of all seeds, yet when it grows, it is the largest of garden plants and becomes a tree, so that the birds come and perch in its branches.'" (Matt 13:31-32)

Give everyone a mustard seed to hold, or another tiny seed. Ask them to think (or talk in groups) about times when they feel that what they do for God is very small. [*For example, many of us feel nervous to speak about God with our friends, or we might think that our actions are too small to make a difference in the world.*]

Remind the group that God takes the tiniest seeds and makes huge trees. Invite everyone to pray, asking God to take their tiny seeds and use them to share his love in the world.

SENDING

Scatter Us, God

Teach the phrase "Scatter us, God", accompanied by hand actions of wiggling your fingers in the air all around, as if they are scattering seeds. Then lead this prayer:

ALL: Scatter us, God,
Leader: to our homes, schools and workplaces.
ALL: Scatter us, God,
Leader: tiny seeds that grow with your care.
ALL: Scatter us, God,
Leader: to share love, truth and encouragement.

ALL: Scatter us, God,
Leader: that your word may bear fruit
in your world.
ALL: Scatter us, God,
Leader: to serve you through our week.
ALL: Scatter us, God,
Leader: and gather us back next week, with stories of your faithfulness.

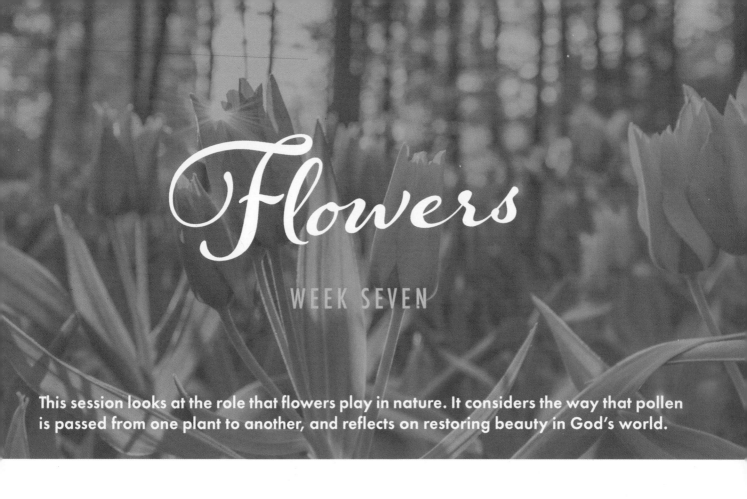

Flowers

WEEK SEVEN

This session looks at the role that flowers play in nature. It considers the way that pollen is passed from one plant to another, and reflects on restoring beauty in God's world.

GATHERING

Colours Song

You can do this as a song (listen to the tune on engageworship.org/ColoursSong) or as a poem - both ways involve interaction. As a leader, sing or say the first line, then point to someone to come up with something of that colour from creation. It might help to have some people who've prepared their answers to start things off. If you're singing it, there is a chorus you can teach.

Explain: Today we're thinking about flowers, and one of the distinctive things about flowers is the bright and varied colours they display. This praise activity helps us think about the variety of colours in God's world.

We're amazed by the blue... [sea/sky?]
And grateful for the white... [snow/polar bear?]
Help us care for the green... [grass/jungles?]
And look after the black... [bears/panthers?]
We're amazed by the red... [flowers/volcanoes?]
And grateful for the grey... [whales/koala?]
Help us care for the pink... [coral/pigs?]
And look after the brown... [wrens/soil?]

God you made them all,
and you made us too,
what a mighty God,
we will worship You.
Give us hearts that love,
give us hands that care,
for the world you made
for us all to share.

Written by the Burr family,
used with permission.

Flower Hunt

Take a walk and look out for flowers. Depending on the time of year, you might find little ones low down on the ground, or big ones high up in the trees, like the ice-cream cone flowers of Horse Chestnut trees.

Get in close and observe what you find. What colours are there? Are the flowers all one colour, or do they blend and combine several? Can you smell them? Does the flower have any insect-visitors right now?

If you like, choose a flower and draw it. Try and capture as much detail as you can.

Be Like a Bee

Explain: There is a reason why flowers are so beautiful, and why they smell lovely. They are attractive in the most literal sense – they are there to attract pollinating insects. It's what they're for.

Insects are drawn in by the smell, the colours, and the tasty nectar that flowers produce. Then when they land, they pick up a bit of pollen from the flower. And a bit of pollen from other flowers gets brushed off. There's an exchange of pollen going on across all the flowers, as bees and other insects hop from one to another. The plants rely on this exchange of pollen to reproduce. Here's a little game to explain.

You will need: a few handfuls of dry foods, kept in separate containers – maybe rice, brown rice, dried beans or lentils, pasta shapes, that kind of thing. This will be the pollen. Now you need some adults to be flowers. They stand in a circle and hold a handful of "pollen" in a hat or in open hands.

Now you need a group of children to be bees. They need to go up to a "flower", take a pinch of "pollen", and take it to another "flower". The aim is for every adult to have a little bit of every kind of "pollen" in their "flower". How quickly can the "bees" do it?

If you want to make it more rowdy, adults can shout out what they're offering, and what they need to complete the set. "I've got beans and I want rice!"

[Please adapt this game if social distancing rules are in place.]

Pass it On

Pollen is a dusty yellow powder, but it also contains the genetic material for the plant – it's like the code that plants need to make more of themselves. So when plants send out flowers to attract bees and insects, they're using those visiting bees as messengers to send each other information.

Form a circle. Whisper a message from one person to another, until it reaches the last person in the line, who says it out loud. Is it the same message as you started with? Let a couple of people have a go at setting a message going, and for the last round, use this phrase: "Pass it on like the beauty of God."

Plants use flowers, in partnership with bees and other insects, to pass along the pollen that they need to multiply.

[If social distancing rules are in place, you can adapt this game by spreading out in a really long line, standing at least five metres away from each other. Each player must then run towards the next person, stopping at two metres and passing on the message as quietly as you can. Talk about how there would be no more flowers if bees and flowers had to socially distance!]

TEACHING

Beauty in the Bible

Explain: God created a beautiful world, and flowers are one of the things in nature that are almost universally loved and admired. Jesus must have liked flowers too.

Ask someone to read:

> "And why do you worry about clothes? See how the flowers of the field grow. They do not labour or spin. Yet I tell you that not even Solomon in all his splendour was dressed like one of these... For the pagans run after all these things, and your heavenly Father knows that you need them. But seek first his kingdom and his righteousness, and all these things will be given to you as well." (Matt 6:28-29, 32-33)

Jesus seems to express a little artistic pride here - "did you ever see anything as beautiful?"

Discuss: If you could wear clothes that looked like a flower, which flower would you choose?

Explain: We see flowers as beautiful. They are colourful and varied, they bring us joy, and it's in God's character to create beautiful things just for beauty's sake. But the beauty of the flowers is also there for a reason, to attract bees and pass on their pollen.

When the Bible talks about beauty, the concept doesn't just mean something that would look good in a photo or on Instagram. In the Old Testament especially, beauty "...at its best was meant to be a reflection of the ordered meaning of God's good creation" (William A Dyrness, *Visual Faith*, page 70).

Things that we describe as "beautiful" are often described simply as "good" in the Old Testament: When it's as God planned it, it's good, it's beautiful! You may remember how many times God called his creation good in the creation story in Genesis.

So, even though we might not admire, for example, a dung beetle in the same way that we admire a bunch of roses, the beetle is beautiful because it's fulfilling the purpose God made it for. And the flower is beautiful, not just because it looks pretty, but because it attracts bees that spread its pollen around, keeping God's creation in balance.

Discuss: Can you think of something that is beautiful because it's good and fulfilling its purpose? [*For example, some might describe intricate technology as beautiful, like the cogs in a clockwork; some describe mathematics as beautiful because of its logic and symmetry; football (soccer) is sometimes known as "the beautiful game".*]

Ask someone to read this passage:

> "While Jesus was in Bethany in the home of Simon the Leper, a woman came to him with an alabaster jar of very expensive perfume, which she poured on his head as he was reclining at the table. When the disciples saw this, they were indignant. 'Why this waste?' they asked. 'This perfume could have been sold at a high price and the money given to the poor.' Aware of this, Jesus said to them, 'Why are you bothering this woman? She has done a beautiful thing to me." (Matt 26:6-10)

Discuss: What does it mean that she did a beautiful thing? Do you know other people who have done beautiful things for God or other people?

RESPONSE

Making the World Beautiful

Use the following example, or another similar illustration that you are aware of. (Pictures on this page from Edible High Town; read more at facebook.com/ediblehightown or edibleluton.org)

Explain: In Luton, a group called Edible High Town received permission to convert disused flower beds (which had become full of rubbish) into community gardens. Local people gathered to clear the trash, dig the soil and plant fruit, vegetables, herbs and flowers.

This not only made the areas physically beautiful, but it also created a beautiful sense of community. Local people could take the produce home for free, to eat, and the environment benefited from bee-friendly plants and greater biodiversity.

Beauty is also often contagious - just like the bees are attracted to the flower because it's beautiful and then go on to pollinate other areas, spreading the beauty, so when one street clears its rubbish, often the next street along gets inspired and does the same.

Discuss: Think about the area you live in, and places that currently lack beauty. What would make those places more beautiful? That could mean removing things that are ugly - cleaning dirt, clearing rubbish or weeds, tidying clutter. It could mean making something look more attractive - painting it, adding flowers or plants, bringing order and neatness. Talk about what is possible and what you might be able to do as a group.

Making your area more beautiful may also mean helping to make it "good" and fit for purpose - what would that look like where you live?

SENDING

Roses are Red

Teach the refrain "roses are red, violets are blue".

Roses are red, violets are blue,
help us to pass on the beauty from you.
Roses are red, violets are blue,
give us a beauty inside that shines through.
Roses are red, violets are blue,
send us to heal, to restore, to renew.
Roses are red, violets are blue,
making things beautiful, in all we do.
Amen.

Fruit

WEEK EIGHT

In this session we explore different kinds of fruit and their function in nature. We learn about the biblical concept of "bearing fruit."

If possible, it would be great to do this session in an orchard (especially a community orchard run by local volunteers). However, it can work just as well in any normal woods or green space.

as we are united in you.
Help us to welcome one another,
support one another
and glorify you in our gathering today,
Amen.

GATHERING

If I Was a Type of Fruit...

Ask people to think about how they are feeling today. If they were a kind of fruit, what fruit would they be and why? For example, someone might be a prickly pineapple because they feel irritable. Or someone might feel sweet and summery like a strawberry, or flat and discouraged like a squashed grape!

Give time for people to think and share. You could ask people to make a shape with their bodies of the fruit they feel like. Then say this gathering prayer:

God, thank you
that however we feel today,
you welcome us.
We are your fruit salad,
all different and all mixed together,
and we celebrate our variety

In an Orchard Activity

Choose one of the trees from the orchard, and observe it. Walk around and take a good look. What are the leaves like? Is there any fruit? Then draw it.

Get back together and talk a bit about your tree – what shape is it? Is it going in all directions or quite 2D? How much fruit is there? Is it straight or wonky? Did you notice anything you hadn't expected?

OR: Fruit Activity

Hand out some fruit you have brought with you (apples, pears and plums would be good, but you could add other fruit too).

Invite everyone to draw one fruit each. Then talk about the different shapes, sizes and colours of the fruits. What is your favourite fruit to eat? Are there any you really don't like?

Fruit Quiz 🧩

[We did this for an orchard growing plums, apples and pears. You could adapt if you have different trees or to make it less UK focussed if you live in another country.]

Give out apple, pear and plum shapes to each person. If you have more time, you could all draw, colour and cut out these shapes as part of the session.

Explain: I'm going to make a statement, and you have to hold up the fruit you think is the correct answer as your vote. Apple, pear or plum? Then we'll see if it's right.

The dried fruit version of this is a prune (Plum)

This is the main fruit used to make cider (Apple)

A popular variety of this fruit is the Victoria (Plum)

There are more than 3,000 varieties worldwide (Pear)

Scientists believe this fruit came out of Central Asia and the Middle East (Apple)

This is closely related to cherries and peaches (Plum)

Both the Ancient Greeks and Romans valued this fruit, and it was associated with love (Pear)

It's thought these were brought to England by the Romans (Pear & plum)

There are 2,500 varieties of this fruit in the UK alone and 7,000 globally (Apple)

The earliest version of this fruit is thought to have come from China and Japan (Plum)

King Henry 8th got his chief fruiterer to find more varieties of this fruit! (Apple)

In 1575, Queen Elizabeth I was so impressed by this tree's beauty she made it an emblem of the city of Worcester (Pear)

Well-known varieties are Conference and Comice (Pear)

In the UK, you harvest these August-September (Plum)

The tree can live for 250 years so the ancient Chinese used it as a symbol of immortality (Pear)

This fruit protects your heart as it has plenty of potassium (Plum)

It can come in the colours, yellow, red, purple, blue and nearly black (Plum)

In Greek mythology, this was seen as a forbidden fruit (Apple)

These trees usually grow to 12 m but can get to 20 m high (Pear)

You harvest these in England August-November (Pear & apple)

TEACHING

Bearing Good Fruit

Have these Bible passages printed out and ask different people to read them. Passage 1:

> "Yes, I am the vine, you are the branches. Those who remain in me, and I in them, will produce much fruit. For without me you can do nothing." (John 15.5-6)

Discuss:

- Why do you think the Bible often uses the image of fruit?

- What does Jesus mean when he says we can "produce fruit"? [*The fruit are the "results" of our faith, the ways we live for God, the choices we make to follow him, to serve others, to care for the world, to share our faith and so on.*]

- What does it mean to "remain in Jesus"? What would that look like practically? [*For example: prayer, reading the Bible, being with other Christians, living God's way...*]

Ask the next person to read passage 2:

> "You did not choose me, but I chose you and appointed you so that you might go and bear fruit – fruit that will last." (John 15:16)

Discuss:

- Which would you rather have, the fruit tree or the fruit it produces? [*Explain how the tree itself isn't good to eat, but the tree is good because it produces the fruit. If you just have an apple, you can only eat it once. If you have a healthy tree, it will keep producing fruit. So really we can't choose between them - we need both the trees and the fruit they produce.*]

- Which would you rather have, a person who believes in Jesus, or a person who does the good things God asks them to do? [*Like the tree and the fruit, we need both. We can't really choose between them. Believing in Jesus is good and healthy when it results in doing the good things God asks. If we just believe but don't act, we are like a tree that doesn't produce fruit. The "fruit" of our believing in God is when we do what he asks us to do.*]

Ask the last person to read passage 3:

> "By their fruit you will recognise them. Do people pick grapes from thorn-bushes, or figs from thistles? Likewise, every good tree bears good fruit, but a bad tree bears bad fruit." (Matt 7:16-17)

Discuss: Do you know someone who bears good fruit? Perhaps it's someone in your group? Encourage one another by sharing stories of Christians bearing good fruit in all sorts of areas of their life.

RESPONSE

Fruit and Seeds

Invite people to eat the fruit you have brought along, and to dig out the pips (which you can explain are actually the seeds of the fruit trees). Talk about how the different fruit taste, and what the different seeds look like.

Discuss: Why do you think these trees surround their seeds with fruit? [*The fruit protects the seeds. It helps the seeds to spread, as animals eat the fruit and either they drop the seeds, or they digest them and then spread the seeds through their droppings.*]

Producing fruit for God in our lives, living the way he calls us to among our friends and family, is a great way to spread the "seeds" of God's Kingdom all around us.

SENDING

Fruit Of The Spirit

We've talked about fruit as the ways we live for God, but the Bible also talks about the "fruit of the Spirit" as the character traits that the Spirit can grow in our lives.

"But the fruit of the Spirit is love, joy, peace, patience, kindness, goodness, faithfulness, gentleness and self-control." (Gal 5:22-23)

Discuss: Which of these would you most like the Spirit to grow in you in the coming weeks?

On your fruit drawing, write the name of the character trait you want the Spirit to grow in you. Pray for each other that God would develop that in you.

Water

WEEK NINE

In this session we learn about the importance of water, both in creation and as a symbol in the Bible. If you have a pond, river or some other water feature near you, you might want to meet there for this session.

GATHERING

He Leads Me Beside Still Waters

Silence and stillness are important parts of worship. You might be surprised how even active children can be still if we give them the chance. People will need to be in a comfortable position, and some may find it easier to have a stick in their hand or something else to fiddle with. Explain that the main goal of this time is just to be still in God's presence, we don't have to achieve anything.

Ask people to join you in saying the line "He leads me beside still waters". Then give a moment's still pause before you say the leader part, before inviting everyone to respond with their repeated line. Repeat, gradually expanding the pause for as long as you think your group can handle it.

He leads me beside still waters. [*Pause*]

He calls me to stop for a moment and rest.
He leads me beside still waters. [*Pause*]

He sees the stressing out and the fraying ends.
He leads me beside still waters. [*Pause*]

The candle burning at both ends.
He leads me beside still waters. [*Pause*]

The core of our being stretched to its limits.
He leads me beside still waters. [*Pause*]

Just for a moment to catch my breath.
He leads me beside still waters. [*Pause*]

Just for two seconds to renew my strength.
He leads me beside still waters. Amen.

Written by Dave Hopwood, used with permission.

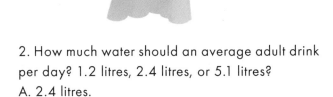

Appreciating Water

Give everyone a glass, or bottle, of water and invite them to take a little sip when you say so.

Say: Water is always on the move. The water in your glass will have been part of icebergs and glaciers. Let's taste the ice.

The water in your glass will also have been part of the sea. Fish have swum through it. It's been hoisted in waves and splashed on the rocks. Let's sip this ocean.

From ocean spray, this water will have evaporated and risen towards the sky on warm air, forming clouds. Let's taste the clouds.

This water has spiralled in almighty storm clouds, fallen as rain, or snow, or hail, or sleet. Let's sip the rain.

Water cannot be destroyed, it can only move from one form to another. So this water in your glass is the oldest thing here. Some scientists think it's older than the earth itself. Let's taste history.

And of course water is the main thing you're made of. Your body is 70% water. It's the main ingredient for making a human being. Let's top ourselves off.

[Clink glasses and say thank you to God for water.]

Who Needs Water? Quiz

If it's not too cold outside, and you want to make it competitive, you can add a watery forfeit for getting a question wrong (for example, a spray with a water gun). Of course, only do this if your whole group is up for it. If you can find an excuse to spray water on any leaders in the group, that's always great fun!

Explain: For each question in this quiz I will give you three options. When I've asked the question, I'll ask you to guess which you think is correct.

1. How much of the human body is water? 10%, 50%, or 70%?
A. 70%.

2. How much water should an average adult drink per day? 1.2 litres, 2.4 litres, or 5.1 litres?
A. 2.4 litres.

3. A drop of water can spend 3,000 years in the ocean before evaporating into the air, how long does the average drop stay in the atmosphere before falling back to Earth? 9 days, 1 month, or 2 years?
A. 9 days.

4. How much water does the average British person use per day? 20 litres, 145 litres, or 4,643 litres?
A. Trick question: 145 litres is how much "direct water" we use out of our taps, but 4,643 litres is how much "virtual water" the average Brit uses each day. This is the water that it takes to make our food, clothes, energy and so on.

5. How many litres of water does it take to grow one avocado? 4.5 litres, 113 litres, or 272 litres
A. 272 litres (this is an example of "virtual water").

6. How many millions of people worldwide don't have clean water close to home? 50 million, 430 million, or 785 million?
A. 785 million.

Explain: Unclean water is one of the major health issues in the world, transmitting diseases such as diarrhoea, cholera, dysentery, typhoid, and polio. Water is impacted by human mistakes such as pollution, pesticides, the effects of climate change and a lack of basic sanitation like toilets and sewage systems.

The earth has its own, natural ways of purifying water. We can see this in spring water, where rain water flows through rocks, sand and soil so that impurities are strained out. We're going to have a go at seeing how this works.

Water Purifier

[Health warning: your purifiers will not leave water bacterially safe to drink. This is just an illustration, do not allow anyone to drink the water.]

Each group will need: Used plastic 2 litre drinks bottle, cut in half, with a hole made in the lid (better to do the cutting and hole-making at home for safety). Coffee filter, cotton wool balls, sand and gravel. Bottle of visibly dirty water.

Get the groups to turn the top half of the bottle upside down. First put in the coffee filter, then the cotton wool, then the sand and finally the gravel. Fit the filled top of the bottle into bottom of the bottle. Pour some dirty water through and see how (visibly) clean it got.

Explain: Beyond this kind of filtering, microscopic organisms also need to be removed. This can be done by boiling the water, and water companies also use high-intensity UV light to disinfect the water we drink. Dr Hilonga from Tanzania recently invented a water filter which uses nanotechnology to absorb things like copper and fluoride as well as bacteria, viruses and pesticides, winning him a prize from the UK's Royal Academy of Engineering for innovation. [engageworship.org/Water_Tanzania]

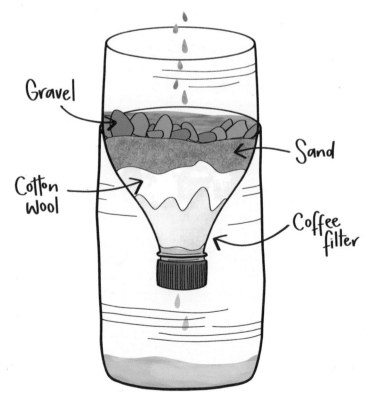

Gravel

Sand

Cotton Wool

Coffee filter

TEACHING

Water in the Bible

Discuss: There are so many references to water in the Bible; let's see how many we can think of. *[Some examples: God separating waters in Genesis 1, Noah and the flood, Moses getting water from the rock, no rain in Elijah's time, water and streams in the Psalms, Jesus by and on lakes, Jesus the water of life, Holy Spirit like streams of water, John baptising, Paul in the storm, River of life in Revelation 22...]*

Discuss: Why do you think water is so important in the Bible? *[For example: It's essential for life. There were no taps so clean water was precious. Water for washing/cleansing of sin. Dangers of travelling by boat and storms. Used as a picture of God's word, refreshing the soul.]*

Explain: Water is a really important image in the Bible. But as well as thinking about it as a picture of a spiritual truth, the Bible also talks about the physical needs the world has for water. When the people of Israel needed water, God provided it. When the land experienced drought, people really suffered. Jesus himself got genuinely thirsty and needed a drink, specifically when he was on the cross. And he talked directly about the need to help people who don't have enough water.

Ask someone to read these verses:

> "'For I was hungry and you gave me something to eat, I was thirsty and you gave me something to drink, I was a stranger and you invited me in...' Then the righteous will answer him, 'Lord, when did we see you hungry and feed you, or thirsty and give you something to drink?...' 'The King will reply, 'Truly I tell you, whatever you did for one of the least of these brothers and sisters of mine, you did for me.'" (Matt 25:35, 37, 40)

Discuss:

- Who are people in the world today who are physically thirsty or hungry due to lack of water?

- What does Jesus mean when he says if we give them a drink, we give a drink to him?

- How does that change our attitude towards helping those without clean water?

RESPONSE

Water and Climate Change

Explain: One of the major factors causing a lack of water is the climate crisis. Climate change is affecting rainfall here and around the world. The world is getting hotter, which means a warmer atmosphere. A warmer atmosphere carries more water vapour. This means that when it does rain here in the UK, we are seeing more heavy rain and flooding.

At the same time, some parts of the world are not getting enough rain, leading to droughts. This means that harvests are failing, people are going hungry and lack clean water to drink. Human activity is driving climate change - how we travel, the ways we make energy, the ways we produce and distribute our food - all of these are currently impacting the global climate. [*For more on this visit* operationnoah.org]

Pray: Let's take some time to pray for these issues. We can ask God to help us change our systems over to renewable energy, to change our diets, to change our habits in what we buy and how we travel. We can pray for both small changes in our own homes and large-scale changes in governments and businesses. [*Pray in small groups.*]

SENDING

God Send the Rain

People can join in with the refrain, "God, send the rain".

Fall on the fields and water the grain,
God, send the rain.
To bring new life to the driest plain,
God, send the rain.
Bring deserts back to life again,
God, send the rain.
Rain healing and strength to those in pain,
God, send the rain.
Rain freedom on those who live in chains,
God, send the rain.
Bring peace where there is war and blame,
God, send the rain.
Father, wash over our sins, and our shame,
God, send the rain.
For this whole world is your domain,
God, send the rain.
And we pray all this in Jesus' name,
God, send the rain.
Aaaa-main!

Birds

In this session we follow in Jesus' footsteps in looking at birds and asking what we can learn from them.

GATHERING

Wings Like Eagles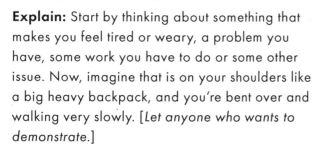

Explain: Start by thinking about something that makes you feel tired or weary, a problem you have, some work you have to do or some other issue. Now, imagine that is on your shoulders like a big heavy backpack, and you're bent over and walking very slowly. [*Let anyone who wants to demonstrate.*]

Isaiah tells God's people that even though we all get tired and weary sometimes, God never gets tired. He promises that when we trust in God, he will renew our strength and we'll soar on wings like eagles.

Can you show me what it would look like to soar on eagle's wings, free and fast? [*Ask those who want to demonstrate.*]

Explain: Now we've practised that, we're going to bring it into prayer. Start off burdened, and slowly become more upright and freer until I say the word "eagles" and then you can really take off with your flying.

"Do you not know?
Have you not heard?
The Lord is the everlasting God,
the Creator of the ends of the earth.
He will not grow tired or weary,
and his understanding no one can fathom.
He gives strength to the weary
and increases the power of the weak.
Even youths grow tired and weary,
and young people stumble and fall;
but those who hope in the Lord
will renew their strength.
They will soar on wings like eagles;
they will run and not grow weary,
they will walk and not be faint." (Is 40:28-31)

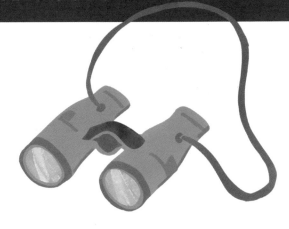

Birdwatching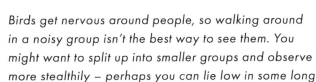

Lead your group on a walk and look out for birds. Pause and listen – what can you hear? How many different bird sounds can you hear? Can you see any of them? Can you match up any birds with their song?

Remind people to look up high in the branches. If there is a pond or a river where you meet, see if there are more birds or different birds there.

Make a note of the birds you see. If you've got a "birder" among you, they can help you to identify any you don't recognise. (Most churches will have a birdwatcher or two if you ask around!) Otherwise you can use a guide book or app.

Hide and Observe

Birds get nervous around people, so walking around in a noisy group isn't the best way to see them. You might want to split up into smaller groups and observe more stealthily – perhaps you can lie low in some long grass, or sit in the branches of an appropriate tree.

If you're lucky enough to be meeting on a nature reserve, there might be a bird hide you can visit.

When you get back together again, exchange notes and see what different groups saw.

TEACHING

Birds of the Bible Quiz

Run this quiz for the whole group where anyone who knows the answer can put their hand up, or divide into teams and write answers on paper. To make it easier, we have given the first letter of each bird. You could omit that and give the Bible reference instead, but that will take longer.

Explain: The Bible mentions dozens of different birds. Some of them are recurring themes, like powerful eagles or gentle doves. But what about pelicans, storks or vultures? Here's a little quiz to explore some of the mentions of birds in the Bible.

1. When Elijah is hiding from his enemies in a cave, which birds beginning with the letter "R" bring him food?
A. Ravens (1 Kings 17:4).

2. In Psalm 102, the Psalmist is lying awake at night feeling lonely. What bird beginning with an "O" do they compare themselves to?
A . "I am like a desert owl, like an owl among the ruins." (Ps 102:6).

3. The prophet Isaiah says that those who "wait for the Lord" will rise up on wings like a bird – which bird beginning with "E"?
A. Eagle (Isaiah 40:31).

4. Which bird, beginning with "H", did Jesus compare himself to when he looked at Jerusalem?
A. A mother hen gathering its chicks (Matthew 23:37).

5. Which two birds did Noah release from the ark to see if it was dry - beginning with "R" and "D"?
A. A raven and a dove (Genesis 8).

6. In the book of Job, which large bird beginning with "O" is called foolish for laying its eggs in the sand and then forgetting about them?
A. An ostrich (Job 39:17).

7. There is a proverb about kings who strut about with their armies. Which strutting bird beginning with "C" does it compare them to?
A. A Cockerel (Proverbs 30:31).

8. Psalm 84 describes birds that are living in the temple in Jerusalem. Which soaring black and white birds beginning with "S" are nesting near the altar?
A. Swallows (Psalm 84:3).

Jesus and the Birds

As Christians, we have chosen to follow Jesus, and we listen to what he tells us. For example, Jesus tells us to love our neighbours. He tells us to share the good news, and to forgive each other. Jesus also tells us to look at the birds.

In the Sermon on the Mount, in Matthew 6, we read these famous words:

> "Do not be worried about the food and drink you need in order to stay alive, or about clothes for your body. After all, isn't life worth more than food? And isn't the body worth more than clothes? Look at the birds: they do not plant seeds, gather a harvest and put it in barns; yet your Father in heaven takes care of them! Aren't you worth much more than the birds?" (Matt 6:25-26)

When we read this passage, it's easy to skip straight to the message about worry and miss the invitation to look at the birds. We might think that Jesus is using the birds as an example, a metaphor for God's care.

But remember that the Sermon on the Mount is called that because it was preached on the side of a mountain. (Yep, Jesus did outdoor worship first!) Jesus was teaching outside, to an audience sitting about on the hillside, so there were probably birds in the sky. When Jesus says 'look at the birds', he might have been able to point at them. His listeners could look and see them for themselves. So it's not just a metaphor. Jesus really does seem to be inviting us to look at the birds.

Discuss:

- What have you gained from following Jesus' instruction to look at birds today?

- What do you think Jesus wants us to learn from the birds in this passage?

- What do we learn here about God's care for the birds, and for wildlife?

- Jesus suggests that watching the birds might help us to worry less. Do you think that might work?

Explain: Scientists have studied the connection between birds and mental health. One study found that people who saw more birds from their windows and in their gardens felt less stressed and anxious. [*If you are interested, follow this up here:* engageworship.org/BirdWatching]

Jesus suggests that when we look at the birds, we see wild creatures being cared for by a generous God. The world isn't a place of scarcity or shortage, where everyone has to grab whatever they can. It's a generous and abundant world, and if we trusted in God's provision we would find that there is more than enough to go around. Watching the birds can remind us of this.

RESPONSE

Care For Birds

Explain: We can work with God in caring for birdlife in our area. There are many things about modern towns and cities which make survival harder for them, but we can do simple things to improve their lives.

Discuss the following things, and what you could do:

- Have you got somewhere in your garden where you could place a birdbox? What about at church? If you've got some DIY enthusiasts, could you run a birdbox-making workshop?

- If you haven't got a bird feeder in your garden, see if there's somewhere you could install one. Keep it topped up and see what new visitors you get.

- Feeding the birds is useful, but you can also grow plants that will provide them with seeds and places to nest. Is there room in your garden or around the church grounds for an elder, hawthorn or rowan? Birds love to hide in ivy too, if you've got a shed or a wall where you could grow some.